RAILS OF CHANGE

TALES OF AN INDIAN RAILWAYS ADVENTURER AND THE QUEST FOR INTEGRITY

AYUSH RANJAN SRIVASTAVA

Made with ❤ on the Notion Press Platform
www.notionpress.com

Dedicated to my parents, family members & Indian Railways

Contents

Preface

As I sit down to write this book, I am reminded of the immense passion that drives me towards both writing and railway. Ever since I was a child, the Indian Railways have always fascinated me. The chugging of the engines, the hustle, and bustle of the stations, the never-ending journey of the trains - all of it left a deep impression on my mind.

It was at the end of my second year of graduation that I realized my true calling - to write a book about the Indian Railways. The railways have been an integral part of our country's history, culture, and economy. It is a vast network of trains, tracks, stations, and people, all working together to transport millions of passengers and goods across the length and breadth of our nation. Through this book, I hope to share my observations, insights, and experiences about the Indian Railways

I am grateful to my parents, who have always provided me with the necessary resources and support to pursue my passion. Their constant motivation and encouragement have been instrumental in shaping me into the person I am today. I sincerely hope that this book will be a delightful read for anyone who shares a love for the Indian Railways

Ayush Ranjan Srivastava
ayushranjan910@gmail.com

INTRODUCTION

Desh ko gati chahiye to bhi rail se milegi aur pragati chahiye to bhi rail se milegi
- PM Modi

Since I first gained consciousness, I have been inexplicably drawn to railways, and my fascination with them has only grown stronger over time. There's something about these towering, metal beasts hurtling through the countryside that captures my imagination and fills me with a sense of awe and wonder.

Despite my best efforts, I have never been able to pinpoint the exact source of this passion. It seems to be an innate part of who I am, a

fundamental aspect of my being that defies explanation or rationalization. There's simply no logical reason for my love of railways - it just is.

Perhaps it's the sheer scale and power of these machines that captivates me. Or maybe it's the sense of adventure and possibility they represent, carrying passengers and cargo to destinations near and far. Whatever the reason, I find myself irresistibly drawn to all things railway-related - from vintage steam engines to sleek, modern bullet trains.

There's a sense of nostalgia and history that comes with railways, too. They've been a part of human civilization for centuries, connecting people and places in ways that were once unimaginable. And yet, even as technology has advanced and other modes of transportation have emerged, railways have endured. They remain an essential part of our world, linking communities and facilitating commerce and travel.

So why do I love railways so much? The truth is, I may never know. But what I do know is that this passion brings me great joy and fulfillment, and I will continue to explore and celebrate the world of railways for as long as I live

As a child, I was deeply enamored with train toys - miniature versions of the towering metal beasts that roared across the countryside. While other kids may have preferred dolls or action figures, I had eyes only for trains. I spent hours upon hours playing with my train sets, laying out tracks, and creating elaborate imaginary worlds for my beloved locomotives to explore.

This fascination with trains spilled over into my everyday life, too. Whenever my family needed to go somewhere, I would insist on travelling by train. I was not interested in any other mode of transportation - not cars, buses, or planes. For me, there was something magical about the way that trains moved, the chugging and whistling of the engines, the clattering of the wheels on the tracks. It was a sensory experience like no other.

My parents, bless their hearts, did their best to accommodate my obsession. They would seek out train-themed destinations and experiences, taking me to railway museums, scenic train rides, and even train-themed restaurants. And whenever we did have to travel by another mode of transportation, they would do their best to make it feel like a train ride - with snacks, games, and activities to keep me entertained.

Looking back, I can see how my love of trains was more than just a passing phase or childhood fancy. It was a deep-seated passion that would stay with me for years to come. Even as an adult, I still feel that thrill of excitement whenever I hear the distant whistle of a train or catch a glimpse of a speeding locomotive. For me, trains will always hold a special place in my heart - a symbol of adventure, possibility, and childhood wonder.

Train rides were always a source of excitement for me as a child - the rush of wind in my hair, the breathtaking scenery flashing by outside the window. But there was one aspect of train travel that filled me with sheer terror - whenever our

train crossed a bridge.

As soon as I saw the bridge looming in the distance, my heart would start pounding in my chest. I knew what was coming next - the deafening roar of the wheels on the tracks, the violent vibrations shaking the entire carriage, the jarring swaying of the train as it crossed the precarious bridge. It was all too much for my young mind to handle.

Despite my best efforts to stay calm, I would inevitably start to cry as soon as the bridge came into view. My parents would do their best to comfort me, assuring me that everything was safe and that we would be across the bridge in no time. But their words did little to ease my fear.

Looking back, I can see how irrational my fear was - after all, train bridges are designed to be strong and sturdy, capable of withstanding the weight and momentum of even the heaviest trains. But as a child, all I could think about was the loud noises and jarring movements that came with crossing the bridge.

Over time, my fear of train bridges gradually lessened. As I grew older and gained a better understanding of how trains and bridges

worked, I was able to view the experience with a sense of awe and wonder rather than fear. Today, I still feel a thrill of excitement whenever I cross a train bridge, but now it's tempered with a sense of appreciation for the engineering marvels that make train travel possible

From a young age, my love for railways was evident to my parents. They saw my fascination with trains and encouraged me to consider a career with the Indian Railways. I was captivated by the idea and decided to appear for the Union Public Service Commission's Special Class Railway Apprentice (SCRA) exam after completing my 12th grade. However, to my disappointment, the exam was abolished in 2016.

Undeterred, I continued my education and completed my 12th grade in 2019. I was considering pursuing a BTech degree when I stumbled upon an exciting opportunity - the Indian Railways had opened its first railway university in Gujarat, called the National Rail & Transportation Institute, now known as Gati Shakti Vishwavidyalaya. Intrigued by the prospect of gaining a deeper understanding of

the transportation industry, I decided to take the entrance examination for admission into the university.

To my delight, I was allotted a place in the Bachelor of Business Administration (BBA) program for rail and transportation management. This course provided me with an in-depth understanding of the transportation industry, including rail transportation, logistics, and supply chain management. The program also included hands-on training in the industry, allowing me to apply my learning in a practical setting.

Though I was initially disappointed by the abolition of the SCRA exam, I felt that I had found a new and exciting path to follow with the National Rail & Transportation Institute. The experience provided me with the tools and knowledge necessary to pursue a career in transportation management and make a meaningful contribution to the industry.

Looking back, I am grateful for the guidance and support of my parents in encouraging me to pursue my passions. Without their encouragement, I may have never discovered the National Rail & Transportation Institute and the opportunities it offered me. I am excited to

see where this career path takes me and to continue exploring my love for railways and transportation

The rail-ways journey

I

The unethical manager/ Gorakhpur railway station

Kishan Kumar, the in charge of the private luggage sanitizing machine located at the main entrance gate of Gorakhpur railway station, approached me with a request. He pleaded with me to take 10,000 rupees and let him go. The urgency in his voice and the nervous look on his face indicated that he was trying to bribe me. This situation clearly showed that Krishan Kumar was indulging in unethical practices and was trying to use the money to escape from the consequences of his actions

On January 5th, the third wave of the COVID-19 pandemic hit, but this time the situation was different from the previous two waves. Despite being a third wave, the number of people who had to be hospitalized and the number of deaths due to the virus were fewer compared to the earlier waves. This could be a result of various factors such as increased public awareness about the virus, better medical facilities, and more effective treatments

I felt a mix of emotions when I arrived back home on the 10th of January. The reason for my return was due to the government's decision to shut down all educational institutions in response to the rapid spread of the Omicron variant of COVID-19. The Omicron variant, which is known to be more contagious than previous strains, had caused concern among the health authorities and they deemed it necessary to take this measure to curb its spread. This sudden announcement came as a surprise to many, including myself. I was expecting to finish the academic year on-campus, but now I had to adjust to remote learning from home. Despite the inconvenience

Indian Railways has taken a proactive step to ensure the safety of its passengers in the wake of the Covid-19 pandemic. In order to prevent the spread of the virus, the railway authority has

requested private companies to install luggage sanitization machines at the primary entrance of major railway stations across the country. The managers of these stalls were instructed to charge a nominal fee of rupees 10 per bag for the sanitization process. This information was clearly displayed on the stall for the passengers to see. However, it is worth mentioning that the luggage sanitization process is not mandatory and is being carried out on a voluntary basis. The Indian Railways are taking all necessary measures to keep their passengers safe and healthy during this pandemic.

As I was feeling extremely bored and unoccupied, I decided to embark on a project to keep myself occupied. My chosen project was based on the Indian railways. The objective of my project was to calculate the passenger inflow and outflow in the terminals of the Indian railways. This would help in understanding the traffic pattern and demand for different routes. Additionally, I aimed to increase non-fare revenue by suggesting new and innovative ideas. This project required a lot of research and data analysis, but I was determined to complete it successfully. I believed that this project would not only keep me occupied but also contribute to the Indian railways in a small way.

I had been feeling quite nostalgic lately and I wanted to reconnect with someone from my past. So, I decided to reach out to Sudhakar, one of my childhood friends. I had not spoken to him in a while, and I was eager to catch up with him. I quickly picked up my phone and dialed his number. When he answered the call, I explained to him that I had a project that I wanted to undertake, and I wanted him to be a part of it. I informed him that I needed him to accompany me to Gorakhpur railway station, where we could discuss the project in detail. I also asked him if he had any suggestions or contributions that he would like to make to the project. I was hoping that he would be as excited about the project as I was, and I was eager to hear his response

Sudhakar and I both agreed to work together on my project. With a common goal in mind, we took a drive to the Railway station to meet the station director, Ashutosh Kumar Singh who holds the title of IRTS (Indian Railway Traffic Service). We felt that meeting the station director would be of great help in achieving our goals for the project

As I made my way through the main entrance of platform number 1, I noticed a strange scene unfolding. The manager of the sanitizing stall was demanding that every passenger pass their luggage through a sanitizing machine before proceeding further. This seemed a little odd to me, as I had never encountered such a scenario before. I soon realized that this was not a standard procedure and that the manager was taking advantage of the situation by illegally charging each passenger a fee of 10 rupees. The passengers, who had no choice but to comply, were visibly upset and frustrated with the manager's behavior. Despite their objections, the manager was unrelenting and continued to force the passengers to pay the fee. This illegal and unethical act was completely unacceptable, and I could not help but feel outraged by the manager's actions.

The amount of Rupees 10 may seem like a small sum, but in reality, it can add up to a significant amount. The Gorakhpur junction is a busy railway station with a passenger traffic of over 250,000 people. On a daily basis, it is estimated that at least 25,000 passengers enter through the main gate. Out of these passengers, it is estimated that 10,000 of them are forced to pay an additional fee of Rupees 10. This results in an illegal daily income of close to 1 lakh Rupees. This may seem like a small amount for an individual, but when multiplied by the number of passengers, it can result in a substantial sum. Despite its small size, this illegal fee can have a significant impact

As I whispered into Sudhakar's ear, I instructed him to capture the entire incident on his phone. I believed that having this recorded evidence could serve as proof in case of any disagreement. Sudhakar quickly took out his high-quality Chinese-made phone from his pocket and started recording the event for a total of five minutes. After the recording was completed, we immediately approached the staff who were overcharging the passengers. Sudhakar initiated the conversation by asking, "Is it necessary for every passenger to sanitize their bags?" The staff replied, "No sir." However, when Sudhakar asked why they were forcing everyone to sanitize their bags, the staff replied that they were merely educating the passengers about the sanitization process. I then interjected, saying, "Don't lie, bhaiya. You're calling back the people who are leaving and forcing them to pay to sanitize their bags." The second staff member attempted to interrupt, but I continued, "Are you sure that you're not forcing them?" At this point, I was so frustrated and angry that I couldn't control myself anymore. I loudly proclaimed that I had recorded the whole incident and that I would be complaining to the higher authorities about the overcharging and coercion. I warned the staff to be prepared for strict actions.

Krishan, the manager of the stall, unexpectedly appeared and offered to help his subordinates. He approached us, me and Sudhakar, with a composed demeanor and suggested that we go to the corner of the stall to have some coffee and snacks. However, Sudhakar was not in the mood to comply and expressed his frustration. He firmly told Krishan that he was not going anywhere and demanded that he say whatever he had to say right there. It was evident that Sudhakar was feeling overwhelmed and wanted to resolve the issue immediately. Despite this, Krishan maintained his calm and tried to diffuse the situation.

Initially, we were reluctant to go along with Krishan Kumar's request to visit the nearby coffee stall. However, as he persisted and repeatedly asked us to accompany him, we finally agreed to take a walk and have a cup of coffee. To be honest, we were not in the mood for coffee but Krishan was quite insistent on the matter. Despite our reservations, we eventually gave in and walked towards the nearby stall to have a sip of the beverage. It was a sudden change of plans but we went along with it anyway. We ended up drinking a cup of coffee which we didn't initially want As we were sipping our hot beverages, Krishan suddenly reached into his pocket and took out his purse.

He leaned in close to me and whispered, "Sir, please keep this 10,000 rupees with you." I was taken aback by his request and asked him what was going on. I was completely bewildered and unsure of what to do. It was the first time in my life that someone had offered me a bribe and that too for a hefty amount of 10000 dollars. I was taken aback by the situation and felt uneasy. However, without even giving it a second thought, I made the bold decision to decline the offer. My moral values and principles were more important to me than any amount of money. I couldn't compromise on my integrity and beliefs just for a momentary gain

I sternly warned Krishan not to engage in any unethical and illegal behavior in the railway premises. Specifically, I made it clear that he should not attempt to bribe anyone again. Bribery is a serious offense and can result in severe consequences such as imprisonment and fines. Krishan was deeply remorseful for his actions of illegally overcharging passengers. He expressed his regret and sought forgiveness for his wrongdoing. He promised me that he would never engage in this illegal behavior again and gave me his word of honor that he would be more responsible and honest in the future. He understood the consequences of his actions and realized the harm he had caused to his passengers. He was determined to make amends and restore trust with his passengers by providing fair and honest service in the future. Krishan's sincere apology and commitment to change were evidence of his sincere remorse and desire to make things right. I told Krishan that I would be visiting this station on a regular basis with the purpose of investigating and monitoring any potential fraudulent activities I made it clear to him that if I encounter any evidence of his involvement in such illegal practices, I will have no choice but to report it to the relevant authorities. My aim is to ensure that the station operates in a transparent and fair manner, and any attempts to compromise the integrity of its operations will not be tolerated. I believe that it is the responsibility of every citizen to protect the interests of the railway station and other government properties, and we should not hesitate to take the necessary steps to uphold these values

After concluding the discussion and putting an end to the matter at hand, my colleague Sudhakar and I came to a decision to cancel our scheduled meeting with the station director Upon reaching this conclusion, we both headed to our respective homes, feeling a sense of relief and accomplishment for resolving the issue my thoughts kept racing with several questions. I couldn't understand why the railway officials, who have their offices right there on the platform, couldn't see the illegal activity happening right in front of them. Were they

blind? I was baffled by the lack of attention and concern shown by these employees. Despite the obvious signs of wrongdoing, they seemed oblivious to what was happening right under their noses. It was a discouraging sight to see that the main entrance of the platform was being used for illegal activities without any action being taken by the railway officials. The station superintendent or deputy station superintendent is responsible for overseeing the security of the railway station. They are granted access to view the live footage from all the closed-circuit television (CCTV) cameras that are installed throughout the station. Despite having this responsibility and access to the live footage, the station superintendent/deputy station superintendent is not taking any actions to address the security concerns of the railway station. This lack of action raises questions about the effectiveness of the security measures in place and the ability of the station superintendent/deputy station superintendent to carry out their duties. It also raises concerns about the safety of the passengers and the property at the railway station. This situation demands an immediate investigation and rectification to ensure the proper functioning of the security system and the accountability of the station superintendent/deputy station superintendent.

II

Journey to the Mumbai division/ western railways

At the conclusion of the first academic year, students at NRTI have the opportunity to participate in internships with Indian Railways. This provides valuable hands-on experience for students to apply the knowledge and skills they have learned in the classroom to real-world situations. The internship program is designed

to allow students to gain exposure to different aspects of railway operations and get a better understanding of the workings of the Indian Railways.To ensure that each student has a personalized experience, students are given the option to indicate their preferred division within the Indian Railways. Based on these preferences, the institution then assigns each student to a specific division, allowing them to work in an area that aligns with their interests and career goals. This approach ensures that each student has a unique and meaningful internship experience that contributes to their professional development.

I was assigned the Mumbai division of Western Railways for a 4- week internship program. I was thrilled to have been selected for this opportunity and couldn't wait to get started. On 2nd August 2021, the internship was set to commence and I was ready to embark on this exciting journey. I was pleasantly surprised to find out that I would not be alone in this experience as seven other individuals had also been assigned to the same division. This was a great opportunity to not only learn from my professors and mentors but also from my peers and to network with them. I was eager to make the most of this chance and was determined to contribute to the division in any way I could.

However, my father was not as happy as I was because this would be the first time I would be leaving home. Initially, my father was not allowing me to visit Mumbai central for my internship and was insisting that I choose the Gorakhpur headquarter instead. . A few days ago, I tried to approach the Gorakhpur headquarter to see if they had any opportunities available, but I did not receive any response from the General Manager/North Eastern Railway. Given the lack of response, I ultimately decided to go with my original choice of the Mumbai division.

My mother was supporting me to join Mumbai division for internship, she was ready to send me to Mumbai and she was also convincing my father. My father agreed after showing a lot of resistance. I was overjoyed at the news and couldn't wait to start my journey in Mumbai. My mother made all the necessary arrangements for my stay and also made sure that I was equipped with all the essentials for my internship. I was grateful for her support and love, without her I wouldn't have been able to pursue my dream.

In addition to the support of my immediate family, other family members also showed their support for my internship opportunity. My cousin brother, in particular, went above and beyond by booking my flight ticket to Mumbai. This was a huge help to me as it saved me from having to endure a long and grueling 35-hour train journey. This act of kindness and generosity meant a lot to me and further strengthened my resolve to work hard and make the most of this once-in-a-lifetime opportunity. My cousin's support not only made the journey easier but also allowed me to arrive in Mumbai well-rested and ready to tackle the challenges that lay ahead.

As she hugged me tightly. My dad and brother tried to comfort her and made sure that I was all set for my journey. The airport was bustling with people and I could hear the sound of the airplanes taking off and landing. I felt a mixture of emotions as I was leaving my family and hometown behind, but at the same time, I was excited for the new adventure that awaited me. My family walked me to the security check and after a final goodbye, I was off to my gate. The flight was on time and I was soon flying high above the clouds, heading towards my destination. As the plane flew over the mountains and rivers, I gazed out the window, bidding farewell to my hometown. The journey ahead was uncertain, but I was ready for it.

Upon arriving at Mumbai at 12:30PM, I was greeted by my uncle who had kindly offered to pick me up from the airport, we took local train from Andheri East railway station (nearest station to airport) to Mumbai central. The experience was a new and exciting one, as I had never traveled by local train before. Mumbai's local train network is one of the busiest and most crowded in the world and traveling on it can be overwhelming, especially for someone who is traveling for the first time. As soon as I stepped into the train, I was struck by how crowded it was. People were hanging out of the doors, and there was barely enough space to breathe. However, I was amazed by how well-organized the system was. Passengers were getting on and off the train with ease, and the train moved at a fast pace. I was also struck by the diversity of people I encountered on the train. People from different backgrounds, cultures, and professions, all traveling together in one crowded compartment. It was a fascinating experience to see people from all walks of life, standing together, yet separate, in their own worlds

Once I arrived at Mumbai Central, I had to report to the Station Superintendent, Mr. Sarwata. He was a kind and welcoming man who immediately offered me a seat and guided me to my designated rest house. I was relieved to find that proper living arrangements had been made for all the interns at the officers' rest house. The officers rest house was a charming and comfortable place to stay. It was fully equipped with all the modern amenities that one could need during their stay. From plush and comfortable beds to a well-equipped kitchen, the rest house was designed to provide a relaxing and homely atmosphere. Additionally, the rest house was situated in a convenient location, near Mumbai central railway station, making it an ideal place to stay This ensured that our stay in Mumbai would be comfortable and stress-free, allowing us to focus on our work and responsibilities without any distractions. Overall, my first local train ride and arrival in Mumbai was a memorable experience, and I was grateful for the hospitality and support provided by Mr. Sarwata.

The next day was a big day for me as I was scheduled to report to ADEN/Poonam Saha, a newly recruited SCRA (Special Class Railway Apprentice) officer who had been assigned to me as my mentor and guide for the duration of my internship. I was feeling a mix of nerves and excitement as I made my way to the office. The then DRM (Divisional Railway Manager), GVL Satyakumar, had carefully chosen ADEN/ Poonam Saha to take on this important role, and I was eager to see what she had in store for me. As I entered the room, I was immediately struck by her energy and dynamic presence. She had a warm smile on her face and was full of positive energy, which immediately put me at ease. Not only was she incredibly knowledgeable about the railway industry, but she was also incredibly beautiful, with a stunning smile that lit up the room. I soon found out that ADEN/Poonam Saha was passionate about her work and dedicated to helping youngsters like me succeed. She spent the next few hours explaining the ins and outs of the railway industry and offering advice on how to approach my internship. She was a true mentor and guide, and I felt grateful to have her by my side as I started this exciting new chapter in my career.

During my internship, I was assigned the task of analyzing the complaints received by the Mumbai division over the past three years. The main objective of my project was to understand the root cause of the complaints and to provide practical solutions to resolve them. The complaint data was collected from various sources, including railmadad (app) , phone calls, and twitter. I then sorted and categorized the complaints based on their type, frequency, and severity. After a thorough analysis, I found that most of the complaints were related to poor customer service, delayed services, and miscommunication between departments

To provide solutions to these issues, I made recommendations to improve customer service and communication channels within the

Mumbai division. I also proposed the implementation of a robust feedback system to monitor and track customer complaints in real-time. The final step was to present my findings and solutions to the management team, along with a detailed action plan to implement the changes. Overall, my internship project was a great learning experience, and I was able to apply the knowledge and skills I acquired in my studies to a real-world problem.

During my internship period, I had the opportunity to go on numerous field visits. To make traveling easier, I was provided with central and western line passes that were valid for a month. This was extremely helpful as it allowed me to explore different areas. Every day, after completing my work, I made it a point to visit Marine Lines. This place was particularly special to me as it was just 2 kilometers away from my workplace. The convenience and beauty of this place made it my favorite destination. I always looked forward to spending some quiet time there after a busy day at work.

As the 4-week internship was officially over and it was time to say goodbye to the city that had been my home for the past few weeks. The memories that I created during my internship were unforgettable, and I would cherish them for the rest of my life. Despite the early morning departure, I was filled with a mix of excitement and sadness as I started my journey back home. The train (Sant Kabir Dham express) from Lokyaman Tilak station was scheduled for 5 AM and I made sure to leave Mumbai Central at 2 AM, so I would have enough time to reach the station and board the train without any hassle. The journey to the station was quite emotional, as I was leaving behind the city that had given me so much in terms of experience and knowledge. My eyes were teary, but my heart was filled with joy, knowing that I would always have these memories to look back on.

The 4 weeks of internship with Indian Railways went by in a flash. For me, the time spent in Mumbai was not just about gaining professional experience, but also about personal growth. I had overcome my fear of being away from home, explored a new city, and made some wonderful memories. The train journey back to Gorakhpur was emotional for me. As the train chugged along, passing through picturesque landscapes, I couldn't help but reflect on the past 4 weeks. I thought about the new friends I had made, the exciting field visits, and the knowledge I had gained. When the train finally pulled into the station in Gorakhpur after 2 days, my family was there to greet me. His mother was overjoyed to see him, tears rolling down her cheeks as she hugged him tightly. His father was also proud of

him for successfully completing the internship and expanding his horizons. I knew that the experience I gained during the internship would stay with me forever and shape myfuture. I felt grateful for the opportunity and promised himself to make the most of every opportunity that came his way. As I settled back into the familiar surroundings of his home, I couldn't help but feel a sense of pride and accomplishment. I was already looking forward to the next chapter of his journey, one that was filled with exciting new opportunities and experiences.

Train management system at Mumbai Central

Board room/ MMCT

The main entrance of Mumbai Central railway station

CSMT railway station

Trip shed/MMCT tour with SSE/elect.

III

The catering scandal/ Maharastra Sampark Kranti story

As we disembarked from the train at Vadodara railway station, the other passengers on our coach erupted into applause. The clapping was deafening. Some of the passengers even stepped off the train to greet us, while others continued to clap and shout slogans from the train's door. The scene was one of jubilation and excitement, with the passengers loudly chanting, "The railway is improving and now it's being put into the hands of hard-working and honest people." The atmosphere was electric, and it was clear that the passengers felt that this was a significant moment for the railway system and for the country as a whole.

The National Rail and Transportation Institute (NRTI) had planned industrial training/ internship for its students to commence in the month of June. The internship committee was making tireless efforts to reach out to a wide range of organizations, with a strong emphasis on government agencies under the Ministry of Railways. This was seen as a crucial opportunity for students from NRTI to gain valuable experience and exposure to real-world work environments.

However, there was an issue that the institute was facing. The position of the Vice-Chancellor was currently vacant. According to the interim arrangement, any officer with the rank of HAG+ in the Indian Railways could hold this position. This situation arose as the previous Vice-Chancellor, Alka Arora Misra, had retired from her post as the Additional Member/HR/Railway Board and as a result, was also removed from the post of Vice-Chancellor. This vacancy was causing some challenges for the internship committee in their efforts to coordinate with organizations for the internships

The task of inviting government organizations to the campus typically fell under the responsibility of the Vice-Chancellor. However, this time around, the job was taken on by the students who were part of the internship committee. These students dedicated their time and effort, working tirelessly to ensure that the invitations were sent out effectively. Some members of the committee were not contributing as effectively as others, and had a tendency to delay tasks and not utilize their time effectively. This likely had a negative impact on the overall productivity and success of the committee, while others were fully committed and hard-working. Also, a couple of members of the committee were occupied with engaging in political maneuvering within their own group rather than focusing on their responsibilities and duties related to the internship program. But, some dedicated students strived to make sure that their efforts produced positive results and that the government organizations received their invitations in a timely and professional manner. Despite the challenges posed by some members who were not fully committed, the internship committee successfully carried out their responsibilities, and their hard work paid off.

The internship committee was facing difficulties in receiving proper responses from the public sector units they were trying to

contact. In order to resolve this issue, I along with my friend Gautam, decided to visit the railway board and meet VG BHOOMA, who was serving as the Principal Executive Director/HR/RB at the time. She was also in charge of the National Rail & Transportation university foundation. She had a great personality and was incredibly intelligent. We had an in-depth conversation that lasted for about an hour, discussing the NRTIs internship program. During our visit, we brought to her attention the challenges we were facing and requested her to exert pressure on the PSUs from the Railway board so that they start responding to us. Our trip to New Delhi took place on March 15th. The outcome of the visit was extremely positive and a couple of memorandums of understanding were signed between NRTI and the PSUs. Our plan was to return to Vadodara on the evening of the 17th via the Maharastra Sampark Kranti express. This train is the fastest non-premium train in India with only 3 stops between Mumbai and Nizamuddin (Delhi).

As the clock struck 4:30 PM, we made our way to the train station, eager to embark on our journey back to Vadodara As we made our way down the aisle, searching for our assigned seats, the hum of chatter and the shuffling of feet echoed throughout the coach. With the train whistle blowing and signaling the departure, we settled into our seats, anticipating the

adventures that lay ahead. The train was cruising at maximum permissible speed and it was 8:30 PM when Gautam, the individual's friend, started feeling hungry. Just at that moment, the IRCTC food vendor came into their coach to take orders for dinner. Since the individual was not hungry, they refrained from ordering any food. However, Gautam ordered a vegetarian meal and paid 120 Rupees for it. He asked the vendor for a bill, to which the vendor replied that he would provide it once the meal was delivered at Kota junction. The train arrived at Kota at around 9:15 PM and the food was delivered to Gautam and other co-passengers. The food was good but the bill was missing. Some passengers asked for the bill but were silenced and reassured that it would be delivered soon. Eventually, everyone fell asleep, and the missing bill was no longer a concern

As someone who has had a lifelong connection to railways, I was getting a feeling that was wrong. Lying on my side in the lower berth of a train, I was lost in memories of my childhood and trying to get some rest. But as it approached 11:45 PM, I decided to check the menu and price list of the food, drinks, and meals being offered on the mail or express trains. To my shock, I discovered that the vegetarian meal that my friend Gautam had ordered was listed at a price of only 80 rupees, yet everyone on the train was paying a staggering 120 rupees. It was clear that the manager of the pantry car had taken advantage of the situation, hiking up the prices by a massive 50% for his own personal gain.

After thoroughly researching the prices on IRCTC (Indian Railway Catering and Tourism Corporation), I attempted to reach the divisional control room by phone. However, due to poor network connectivity, I was unable to connect my call. This setback caused me to take matters into my own hands and I immediately headed towards the pantry car to confront the manager. Upon arriving, I found the manager fast asleep, which further fueled my frustration. I woke him up by shaking his hand in anger and began to scold him for overcharging the passengers. I demanded to see the register, where the manager kept record of all the passengers who had ordered food on the train, to verify his claims.

Upon confirming the facts, I instructed the manager to accompany me and refund the surplus amount to all the customers who had purchased food. The manager was visibly trembling and appeared to be petrified, he obeyed my directives without hesitation. I accompanied him as we went from one passenger to another, returning their overpaid money. The gesture was met with great appreciation from the majority of the passengers, who were overjoyed with the outcome. The manager's fear slowly subsided as he saw the satisfaction of the passengers and realized that everything was going to be okay. By the end of the process, the manager had a newfound sense of confidence, knowing that he had taken the right steps to rectify the situation.

I took a strong stance and communicated my concern to the manager. I also alerted the divisional control room of the situation. Upon arriving at the Vadodara railway station, all of the passengers in my compartment were elated and gave my friend Gautam and I a standing ovation. For a brief moment, they shouted out slogans, expressing their approval and admiration for the honest and hardworking individuals now in control of the Indian Railways. This incident may have had a positive impact on public perception and changed the way some people view the employees and officers working for the Indian Railways.

It is imperative that everyone exercise caution when making purchases within railway premises. Before making a transaction, it is crucial to verify the maximum retail price of the item in question to avoid being overcharged. If you suspect that you have been a victim of cheating or overcharging, there are several ways to report this. You can contact the control room

by dialing the number 139, or by registering a complaint on the Railmadad platform or Twitter. This will ensure that your grievances are heard and appropriate action is taken to rectify the situation. By taking these simple steps, we can ensure fair and just dealings within railway premises and protect the rights of all passengers.

My confrontation with the pantry car manager resulted in the discovery of a larger scam being run by the IRCTC vendor. The manager was found to have been overcharging passengers on multiple trains, taking advantage of their trust and ignorance. The individual reported the matter to the railway authorities and an investigation was launched. The manager was eventually fined.

This experience also taught me the importance of being vigilant and taking matters into our own hands when necessary. I learned that it was possible to bring about change and make a difference, even in a large organization like the Indian Railways. The experience left a lasting impact on me.

The incident could have influenced people's perceptions and attitudes towards Indian Railways in positive ways

IV

The IRFCA convention/ Siliguri & Darjeeling

IRFCA is a digital platform that serves as a forum for numerous train enthusiasts who are specifically fascinated by the railway systems in India, and it also has affiliations with other railfan communities worldwide. The group has been instrumental in advancing and safeguarding the diverse past and legacy of Indian railways, as well as supporting the expansion and evolution of railfanning as a recreational pursuit in India. IRFCA conventions are typically held in the month of February each year and last for 2-3 days. The

conventions offer a variety of activities and events for railfans to participate in. Field trips to railway stations and heritage sites are often organized, providing enthusiasts with the opportunity to observe and photograph trains and railway infrastructure up close. Presentations and talks by experts and fellow railfans cover a range of topics related to railways, such as history, technology, and operations. Quizzes and other games are alsoorganized, allowing railfans to test their knowledge and compete against one another.

IRFCA conventions also serve as a platform for enthusiasts to network with one another, share their experiences, and discuss their common interests. In addition to the official events, there are often informal gatherings and social activities, such as dinners and socializing sessions, which allow railfans to connect with one another on a personal level. Overall, IRFCA conventions are a great way for railway enthusiasts to come together and celebrate their shared passion for railways, while also learning more about the history, technology, and culture of India's railways

In September 2021, Sourya Basu, a friend of mine, shared exciting news about the IRFCA convention 2022. The convention was scheduled to take place on 13-14th February in Siliguri and Darjeeling. I was a railfan, and along with three other friends, Vivek Rajeev, Adishwaran Konar, and Sourya Basu, we shared interest in railways. We all planned to attend the 2022 convention, and our excitement was palpable, especially because it was going to be our first IRFCA convention. Attending the IRFCA convention would give us the opportunity to meet other railfans and learn more about our passion for railways. We were looking forward to attending talks, presentations, and workshops that would be conducted by experts in the field. In addition, we were excited about the prospect of visiting Siliguri and Darjeeling, two beautiful locations that were famous for their scenic railway routes. The convention would provide us with an opportunity to explore the local culture, cuisine, and traditions.

We, I, Sourya Basu, Vivek Rajeev, and Adishwaran Konar, had a time constraint due to our classes scheduled in the second week of February. As a result, we decided to split our journey, taking a flight for one leg of their journey and returning via train.

In January, we all 4 booked our flight tickets from Ahmedabad to Bagdogra (Siliguri) for the IRFCA convention 2022. We were excited about attending the convention and exploring the scenic locations in Siliguri and Darjeeling. Despite the COVID-19 pandemic, we were confident that the convention would take place as scheduled. We had heard that the second wave of COVID-19 had ended, and there were no visible signs of the third wave at that time. We were also aware that the IRFCA would take all necessary precautions to ensure the safety of attendees, such as mandatory masks and social distancing.

Unfortunately, a few weeks after we had booked their flight tickets for the IRFCA convention 2022, the third wave of COVID-19 started to emerge. Cases began to rise in several states, including West Bengal, where Siliguri is located. As a result, the West Bengal government started assessing the situation and decided to impose restrictions on public gatherings beginning from the last week of January. These restrictions were put in place to curb the spread of the virus and prevent further transmission. We became increasingly concerned about the situation and the possibility of the IRFCA convention being canceled or postponed. We wondered whether they would still be able to attend the convention and whether it would be safe to do so. Despite our concerns, we kept a close eye on the situation and hoped that the convention would still be held as scheduled. We knew that the IRFCA would take all necessary precautions to ensure the safety of attendees, and we were eager to attend the convention and experience the scenic train rides in Siliguri and Darjeeling. Our excitement turned to disappointment when we learned that the convention dates were being postponed due to the third wave of COVID-19 and the government restrictions on public gatherings. Although we were disappointed, but the decision to shift the convention dates was a good one. We understood the risks involved, especially considering that many older railfans also attend the convention. The health and safety of everyone involved were of utmost importance. We were saddened by the news, but they knew that it was for the best. We decided to cancel their flight tickets with heavy hearts, knowing that they would miss out on a unique opportunity to meet fellow railfans and learn more about their shared passion.

****

After the disappointment of the IRFCA convention 2022 being postponed due to the third wave of COVID-19, we were delighted to learn that the convention would be rescheduled for the 30th of April and the 1st of May. The venue remained the same, and the convention promised to be an exciting event once again.

However, two of the friends, Sourya and Vivek, opted out of attending the convention for some reason. This left only two of us Adishwaran and me, to plan everything Accordingly. We faced a challenge in finding a direct connection from Vadodara to Siliguri. After some research, we decided to take a train from Ujjain, a nearby city that had a direct connection to Siliguri. We booked our tickets in DADN KYQ (19305) from Ujjain in 2nd AC. The waiting list for our tickets was 7, but we were confident that our tickets would easily get confirmed. However, as the departure date approached, the waiting list remained at 7. We started to worry that they might not be able to attend the convention after

all. One day before the departure of the train, we were disappointed to see that the waiting list was still at 7.

After waiting for a long time and seeing no change in the waiting list status of our DADN-KYQ train tickets, I and Adishwaran made a difficult decision to cancel our tickets. We did not want to risk not being able to attend the IRFCA convention 2022 in Siliguri and Darjeeling. After some brainstorming and research, we came up with a new plan. We decided to take the Golden Temple Mail from Vadodara to New Delhi, which had better connectivity options, and then take the Rajdhani Express from New Delhi to Siliguri. We immediately booked our tickets in the Golden Temple Mail and requested the Senior Divisional Commercial Manager (Sr DCM) to put our tickets in EQ quota due to the high waiting list. EQ quota is an emergency quota that is reserved for last-minute ticket bookings for emergency travel, and is usually allocated to senior railway officials. Fortunately, our request was approved, and tickets were confirmed after the chart preparation.

We boarded the train from Vadodara to New Delhi. We reached the New Delhi Railway Station at around 2 PM and went to Yamuna Officers Rest House, which was situated nearby.

However, while we were resting, we received a notification that their Rajdhani Express train had been cancelled for that day due to unforeseen circumstances. The news left us feeling anxious and uncertain about how we would reach Siliguri. We immediately started to explore alternate travel options to reach Siliguri. We tried to look for trains that were available, but unfortunately, all of them

were already fully booked or had long waiting lists. As we explored our options, we checked trains from nearby major locations and were surprised to find that seats were available on the same train we had initially booked from Ujjain Junction to Siliguri. This train was the DADN KYQ Express, and the available seats were in the current quota for 3rd AC. We were thrilled to find this alternative option and quickly booked our tickets on the DADN KYQ Express for the remainder of our journey. We were relieved to have secured confirmed seats and finally had a reliable plan to reach Siliguri in time for the convention. There was still the challenge of getting to Lucknow from New Delhi in time for the 4 AM departure of the DADN-KYQ express. The next available train to Kanpur (70km from Lucknow) was the Shivganga Express at 8PM, but we had no tickets. We decided to take our chances and headed to the railway station at 7:30PM. As we arrived, we saw the Shivganga Express standing on the platform with its powerful WAP 7 locomotive in the lead. The train was fully packed, and we knew it was going to be a challenge to find seats. We approached the TTE and explained our situation, telling him that we were from the Railway University and needed seats till Kanpur. The TTE sympathetically replied that there were no available seats due to the crowded train, but if we happened to find any vacant seats, we could occupy them. Without any other options, we boarded the S6 coach of the train. It was difficult to navigate through the throngs of passengers, but we managed to find a small space to stand near the washroom. We were not alone, as several other passengers were also standing due to the lack of seats. Despite the crowded conditions, we were determined to reach Kanpur on time. We spent the next 5 hours standing, occasionally shifting our position to alleviate the discomfort. As the train approached Kanpur, we kept a close eye on our watches, hoping that we would arrive on time.

Finally, after what felt like an eternity, the Shivganga Express pulled into Kanpur Central. We quickly disembarked and went to bus station to take next available bus to Lucknow junction After our harrowing experience in trying to find an alternate route to Siliguri, we finally boarded our final train, the DADN-KYQ express from Lucknow. Despite being delayed by an hour, we were grateful to finally have a confirmed ticket and a train to take us to our destination. We quickly settled into our respective berths and soon fell asleep, exhausted from our long and stressful journey. When I woke up several hours later, I realized that my clothes were emitting a strong odor due to the sweat and dust that had accumulated on them the previous day. I immediately changed into fresh clothes and felt much better. As the train chugged along, we passed through the town of Ballia, and I marveled at the sights and sounds of rural India. However, our peaceful journey was soon disrupted by a series of chain pullings by some miscreants. It was disheartening to see such behavior and the inconvenience it caused to other Passengers. Unfortunately, our troubles were not over yet. The train reached Barauni Junction 3.5 hours behind schedule, due to the chain pullings in the eastern part of Bihar. We were worried that our further journey to Siliguri might be impacted by this Delay. As our train crossed Katihar Junction, we noticed that it would come to a halt every 15 minutes. After a while, we realized that there was a problem with the brake pipe, and air pressure was leaking. The frequent stops further delayed our journey, and we finally arrived at Siliguri at 7:30 AM, more than five hours late than our scheduled arrival time of 2 AM. We were already behind schedule, and the delay made us even more nervous as the convention was slated to begin at 8:30 AM. We knew we had to move quickly and reach our hotel as soon as possible. As soon as

we reached Siliguri, we gathered our belongings and hastened to the hotel.

****

The Milestone hotel in Siliguri was the designated venue for the convention that we were attending. It was a bustling hub of activity, with people from all over the country gathering to participate in various events and activities. As soon as we arrived at the railway station, we made our way to the hotel to check-in and settle in. The hotel staff warmly welcomed us with open arms and provided us with traditional shawls, as well as a few other goodies like a diary, tea bags, and mugs. It was a heartwarming gesture that made us feel right at home. After the warm greetings, we were escorted to our hotel rooms where we could finally rest for a few minutes. The rooms were spacious, comfortable, and equipped with all the modern amenities one could ask for. The beds were plush and inviting, and we couldn't wait to sink into them after a long day of traveling. As we settled into our rooms, we took a moment to admire the stunning views outside our windows. The lush greenery of the surrounding hills, the hustle

and bustle of the city below, and the serene beauty of the landscape were all breathtaking. We couldn't have asked for a better venue to host our convention Once we freshened up, we made our way to the hotel restaurant for a hearty breakfast to fuel ourselves for the busy day ahead. With our stomachs full and our minds eager, we set out for the convention. The convention was a lively affair with several presentations and guest lectures by industry experts, including DRM Katihar. We learned a great deal about the latest developments in the field of transportation, and it was fascinating to hear from people who had dedicated their lives to the railway industry. After a busy morning, it was time for a well-deserved break. We were all excited to embark on our toy train ride, which was a highlight of the convention. We boarded a bus to the nearest toy train station, which was Sukna, and soon we were on our way aboard a charming little train with three coaches. The narrow gauge train chugged along at a leisurely pace, and we were able to take in the stunning scenery around us. The lush green hills, the tranquil forests, and the picturesque villages all made for a magical experience. The fresh mountain air was invigorating, and we all felt rejuvenated by the end of the ride. We also got the opportunity to explore the NG shed of Tindharia, where we learned about the rich history of these little trains. It was fascinating to see the different locomotives and carriages that had been used over the years, and we gained a newfound appreciation for the hard work and dedication that went into maintaining these charming little trains. Overall, the toy train ride was an unforgettable experience that added a touch of magic to our convention. We returned to the hotel with a renewed sense of enthusiasm and wonder, grateful for the opportunity to be part of such a special event. The day was far from over, and there were several other field trips planned for the delegates. However, despite my excitement, my body was beginning to tire, and I could feel my eyelids drooping. I knew that I needed to rest if I wanted to fully enjoy the remaining activities. With a heavy heart, I excused myself from the group and made my way back to my hotel room. As soon as I lay down on the soft, inviting bed, I drifted off into a deep and restful sleep. I slept for a couple of hours and woke up feeling refreshed and re-energized. I was disappointed to have missed out on some of the day's events, but I knew that taking care of my body was important, especially during a busy event like the convention. As I got ready to head back to the convention, I reflected on the importance of self-care and how taking the time to rest and recharge can have a significant impact on our ability to enjoy and engage with the world around us. Despite missing out on some of the field trips, I was able to catch up with some of the other delegates and learn about their experiences. I was grateful to be part of such a supportive and engaging community, and I knew that the memories and connections I

made during the convention would stay with me for years to come.

The next day, which was May 1st, was a big day for me as I was scheduled to give a presentation. Along with my presentation, there were a few other events such as quizzes and guest lectures that were also planned. I was feeling both excited and nervous as I prepared for my turn to take the stage. When it was finally my turn, I took a deep breath and stepped up to the podium. I delivered my presentation with confidence and enthusiasm, and the audience responded with a round of applause. It was a wonderful feeling to be able to share my ideas and insights with such an engaged and supportive group of professionals. After my presentation, I had the opportunity to interact with some of the other distinguished leaders attending the convention. I was honored to meet with individuals like Ganesan Raghuram, the former director of IIM Ahmedabad, Dheeraj Sanghi, the Vice Chancellor of LP University and former dean of IIT Kanpur, and Saket Modi, a senior software engineer at Google. Being able to connect with such accomplished and experienced individuals was an incredible opportunity, and I felt grateful for the chance to learn from their wisdom and expertise. Overall, the convention was a truly memorable

experience, full of learning, networking, and personal growth. I felt inspired and energized by the passionate and committed community of railway professionals, and I knew that I would carry the lessons and insights from the convention with me for the rest of my career

On the afternoon of 1st May, it was time for us to bid farewell to Siliguri and head back home. Adish and I grabbed a quick lunch before making our way to the railway station. We were scheduled to take the Sikkim Mahananda Express, which would take us to Kanpur. From there, we had planned to catch the CNB-ADI Special Express, which would take us all the way to Vadodara. We had made all the necessary bookings and arrangements in advance, so we were all set for our journey. As we boarded the train and settled into our seats, I couldn't help but feel a sense of nostalgia wash over me. The convention had been an unforgettable experience, and I was grateful for all the wonderful memories that I had made during my time in Siliguri. Despite the fatigue and exhaustion that I was feeling, I couldn't help but feel a sense of excitement at the thought of returning home and sharing my experiences with my friends and family. As we chugged along on the Sikkim Mahananda Express, I spent some time reflecting on the past few days.

From the informative presentations and guest lectures to the fun field trips and interactions with esteemed professionals, it had been a truly enriching experience. I felt grateful for the opportunity to be a part of such a fantastic event and to learn so much about the world of railways and Transportation. Finally, after a long and tiring journey, we arrived in Vadodara on the morning of 3rd May. As we stepped off the train and made our way out of the station, I couldn't help but feel a sense of accomplishment. The convention had been a great success, and I felt proud to have been a part of it. As I headed home, I knew that I would always cherish the memories of my time in Siliguri and the valuable lessons that I had learned during the convention.

1st-time IRFCA convention attendees

Group photo

Tindharia workshop

Toy train ride

Flatbed (attached to toy train)

Sukna raikway station

Inside building (Sukna railway station)

Bus ride to Sukna

SUKNA
प्रथमश्रेणी प्रतीक्षालय
FIRST CLASS WAITING ROOM
DARJEELING
HIMALAYAN RAILWAY

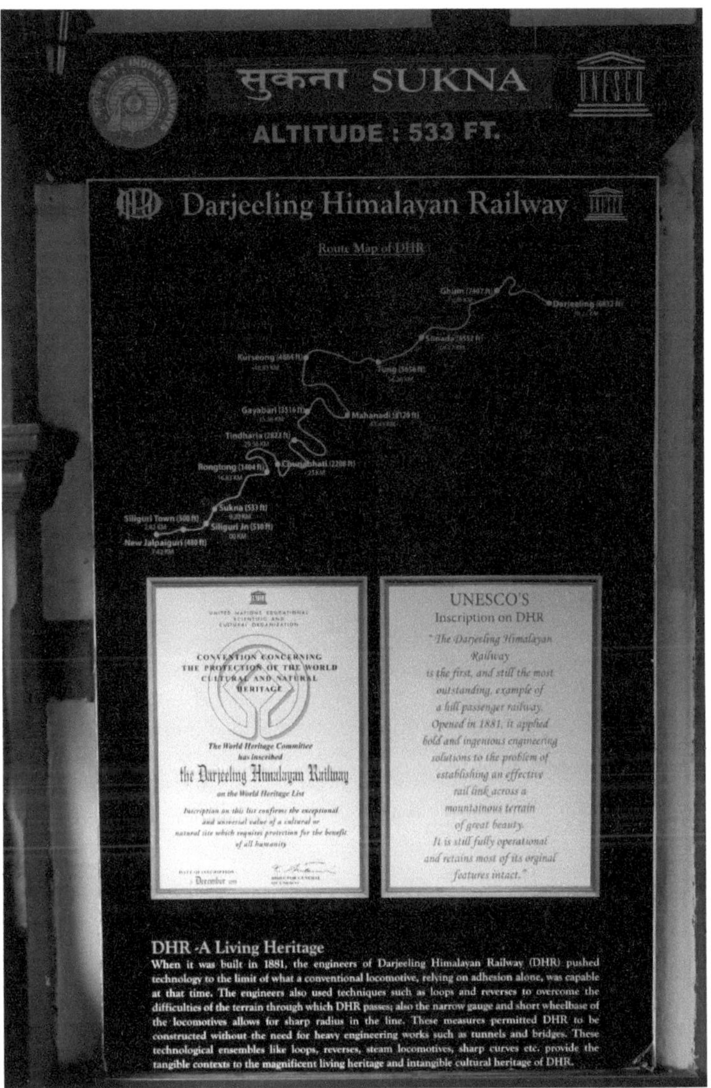

सुकना SUKNA
ALTITUDE : 533 FT.
Darjeeling Himalayan Railway
Route Map of DHR
UNESCO'S
Inscription on DHR
"The Darjeeling Himalayan
Railway
is the first, and still the most
outstanding, example of
a hill passenger railway.
Opened in 1881, it applied
bold and ingenious engineering
solutions to the problem of
establishing an effective
rail link across a
mountainous terrain
of great beauty.
It is still fully operational
and retains most of its orginal
features intact."
CONVENTION CONCERNING THE PROTECTION OF THE WORLD CULTURAL AND NATURAL HERITAGE
The World Heritage Committee
has inscribed
the Darjeeling Himalayan Railway
on the World Heritage List
DHR -A Living Heritage
When it was built in 1881, the engineers of Darjeeling Himalayan Railway (DHR) pushed technology to the limit of what a conventional locomotive, relying on adhesion alone, was capable at that time. The engineers also used techniques such as loops and reverses to overcome the difficulties of the terrain through which DHR passes; also the narrow gauge and short wheelbase of the locomotives allows for sharp radius in the line. These measures permitted DHR to be constructed without the need for heavy engineering works such as tunnels and bridges. These technological ensembles like loops, reverses, steam locomotives, sharp curves etc. provide the tangible contexts to the magnificent living heritage and intangible cultural heritage of DHR.

V

The window seat dilemma/Double Decker Express

After completing my 11th grade, I had a brief break of a couple of days before commencing my 12th grade. Specifically, my 11th grade concluded on February 24th, marking the end of that academic year. During break time, as I sat pondering about my plans for the next few days, I suddenly got the urge to visit my uncle in New Delhi. Having not seen him in quite some time, I thought it would be a great opportunity to catch up with him and spend some quality time together.

My father, being well-connected in the Indian Railways, booked my train ticket on the prestigious Vaishali express. This train is known for its comfortable and luxurious amenities and is one of the most sought-after modes of transportation for passengers traveling between Saharasa in Bihar and New Delhi. Due to its popularity and high demand, it is often quite difficult to secure a ticket on the Vaishali express, particularly during peak travel periods. However, my father was able to secure a confirmed ticket for me, despite the high waiting list of passengers and the crowded conditions that often prevail on the route between Gorakhpur and New Delhi. This was made possible by his connections and his access to the VIP quotas that are reserved for high-ranking officials and other privileged individuals. As I boarded the train and settled into my comfortable seat, I felt grateful to my father for his efforts in securing my ticket on the Vaishali express

During my visit to New Delhi, I had the chance to experience the vibrant culture of the city. I visited iconic landmarks like the India Gate, the Red Fort, and the Lotus Temple. I also indulged in the delicious street food that the city is famous for, including chaat, chole bhature, and kebabs. The local markets, such as Chandni Chowk and Connaught Place, were a treat to explore and I found some amazing souvenirs to take back home. I even had the opportunity to meet some friendly locals who shared their stories and insights about the city with me. However, as much as I enjoyed my time in the capital, it was time for me to return to Gorakhpur

As I was planning my trip back home, I knew that my aunt had expressed a keen desire to visit my mother, whom she had not seen in a long time. Given that Lucknow was on the way, I decided to split my return ticket into two parts, so that I could easily pick her up on the way and ensure that she could fulfill her wish. Although it meant a slight inconvenience in terms of additional planning and expense, I knew that it would be worth it to see the happiness on my mother's face when her sister arrived. Additionally, I was also looking forward to spending some quality time with my aunt during the journey back home and catching up with all that had been happening in her life since we last met. All in all, the decision to book the return ticket in 2 parts was a small sacrifice to make for the sake of family bonding and creating unforgettable memories. The journey back home was divided into two parts. The first part of the journey was scheduled from Anand Vihar to Lucknow, and it was a double-decker express. The 2nd part was in Lucknow Barauni express from Lucknow to Gorakhpur

At precisely 2:00 PM, I was set to embark on my journey from Anand Vihar via a double-decker train, with an estimated arrival time of 10:00 PM in Lucknow. In preparation for my journey, my thoughtful aunt had prepared a scrumptious dinner for me, ensuring that I wouldn't have to go hungry. Grateful for her kindness, I eagerly awaited the moment when I could finally dig in. My uncle had kindly offered to drop me off at the station and managed to arrive just five minutes before the train's scheduled departure. I quickly gathered my belongings and hurried towards the platform, hoping to catch the train in time. Without further delay, I boarded the train and set off on my adventure Upon boarding the train, I discovered that someone was already occupying the window seat I had been assigned. Although the aisle seat was empty, I hesitated for a moment before deciding to take it instead. My assumption was that the individual in my assigned seat would quickly realize their mistake and relocate to their own assigned aisle seat. However, as the minutes ticked by and the train continued to fill up with passengers, the individual remained in his seat by the window. As the first hour of my journey passed, my apprehension continued to grow. I couldn't help but notice that the man sitting next to me had unknowingly taken up the seat that I had specifically chosen, my beloved window seat. As an introverted individual, I found it difficult to summon the courage to speak up and politely request my seat. However, as the journey drew to a close, I found myself filled with regret for not asserting myself. The thought of spending the entire journey without my coveted window view filled me with disappointment. Throughout the duration of the trip, my mind was consumed with indecision, questioning whether or not to speak up and ask for what was rightfully mine. Alas, I allowed my timid nature to prevent me from advocating for myself, ultimately resulting in a journey that was less than satisfactory

Finally, after enduring a rather unsatisfying train journey, I arrived in Lucknow at 2355 hours. Unfortunately, the train was delayed by approximately two hours due to some issues with the EOG coach. Nevertheless, the issue was promptly resolved and the EOG was replaced at the Moradabad junction. Despite the delay, I was relieved to have arrived safely.

The lesson to be learned from this story is to assert yourself and speak up for what you want and what is rightfully yours. Being timid and not advocating for yourself can lead to dissatisfaction and missed opportunities. It's important to have the courage to assert yourself, especially in situations where your desires or needs may be overlooked or ignored

Finding my platform

VI

Intimidation: A Story of Harassment and Revenge

I was experiencing persistent harassment from a 20-year-old boy named Unmukt Kumar who was a student at one of the prestigious schools in Gorakhpur. He was constantly testing my limits and subjecting me and my then-girlfriend Vani to abusive language. Both Vani and Unmukt attended the same school. This behavior was causing great distress for me and Vani and was making it difficult for us to carry on with our daily lives. Despite our attempts to make him stop, Unmukt persisted with his threats and insults, making us feel intimidated and helpless.

It was a traumatic experience for both of us, and we were in need of help to put an end to this behavior.

Unmukt, who was previously just a friend, began to experience romantic feelings for Vani. He was aware of the fact that Vani and I were in a relationship, but he believed that I was an introverted person who would not take any actions against him. Despite knowing that Vani was already in a relationship, Unmukt couldn't help but feel drawn towards her. He knew that his feelings might create complications in the relationships, but he couldn't suppress them. Unmukt was struggling with the dilemma of whether he should pursue his feelings or stay away and let Vani and I be together. However, he remained confident that my introverted nature would keep me from making any moves against him.

One day, I was fully engaged in my coaching classes, learning the intricate details of coordinate geometry. My attention was solely focused on the lecture when my phone rang continuously. I noticed that the caller was my girlfriend, Vani, but I decided to ignore her calls and concentrate on the class. During the break time, I finally called Vani back to find out what was going on. To my surprise, she was extremely nervous and seemed to be on the verge of tears. She revealed that her friend, Unmukt, had proposed to her and had asked her to end our relationship. I could sense the discomfort and nervousness in her voice, and I knew that this situation was going to be difficult for both of us.

I was completely stunned when I heard the news. I couldn't believe what I had just learned. After the class was over, I immediately went home and called my friend Vani. I asked her about the situation and told her to tell Unmukt that she was in a relationship and if he didn't listen to her, she should start ignoring him. After our conversation, she agreed to do what I asked. From that moment on, Vani stopped talking to Unmukt. I was a bit worried about the outcome

Unmukt was deeply hurt by Vani's rejection and instead of dealing with his emotions in a mature manner, he chose to take his frustration out on her by defaming her. He spread false rumors and indulged in malicious gossip, causing immense harm to Vani's reputation. Despite all this, Vani remained patient and tolerant, trying her best to ignore his actions. However, one day, Unmukt went too far. He started hurling abuses at Vani, crossing the line of acceptable behavior. Faced with this unbearable situation, Vani confided in me about what was happening. I offered her some advice, telling her to not let Unmukt's actions affect her and to stay focused on her studies. I emphasized the importance of not letting such negative people impact her life and instead, to keep moving forward towards her goals.

A few days had gone by and one day, I received a call from Unmukt. He spoke to me in a challenging tone, saying, "If you're brave enough, come to my school today and I'll make you remember your grandmother." I was taken aback by his statement and I immediately called my friend Nakul Kumar, He had a criminal mind. He was a giant of a man, standing at an imposing 7 feet tall. His height alone was enough to intimidate anyone who crossed his path, and combined with his criminal mindset, it made him a force to be reckoned with. He was known for his cunning and ruthless nature, often getting what he wanted through any means necessary. Despite his criminal tendencies, he was always there for me when I needed him, and I will never forget his friendship and loyalty.Nakul was more inclined towards hooliganism than academics. I quickly told him about the situation and described the entire incident to him. Nakul was eager to help me out. He knew that I needed support and he was ready to stand by my side no matter what. I was grateful for his willingness to help, and I knew that I could count on him to have my back.

The following day, I made my way to Nakul's home. Upon arrival, I was greeted by six boys who were waiting with Nakul for my arrival. We were all eager to head off to LFS School. I was nervous as we headed towards the school. Nakul and I hopped on our scooty while the other boys mounted their bikes. We then set off towards the main gate of LFS School, driving down the road together as a group. The sound of the engines revving filled the air as we made our way towards the school. We were all eager and were looking forward to the drama that awaited us at LFS.

After reaching the school, I signaled all of my friends to stay back, so that Unmukt wouldn't feel intimidated by the fact that Ayush had brought along six people to attack him. After a

few minutes, I finally saw Unmukt approaching me with a confident, almost arrogant demeanor, reminiscent of Bollywood star Shah Rukh Khan. I walked towards him, feeling my heart racing with a mixture of fear and anger. As we got closer, I reached out and gave him a hard slap across the face, followed quickly by Nakul, who punched him in the face. The force of the blow caused Unmukt to stumble backwards, and I could tell by the look on his face that he was both surprised and intimidated. Despite my initial fear, I felt a sense of satisfaction knowing that I had stood up to him and made my point.

Unmukt was in shock as he rubbed his cheek, trying to process what had just occurred. He had just been slapped a few times and was trying to figure out what led to this sudden attack. His mind was racing, trying to recall the events that had taken place leading up to the altercation. He was feeling confused and bewildered, wondering what could have possibly triggered such an aggressive reaction from the person who had just slapped him. He knew that he had to get to the bottom of this and find out what had gone wrong, so he took a deep breath and started to piece together the events that had led to this sudden altercation

We hopped into our bikes and started our engines. The adrenaline rush was still high and we couldn't help but feel a sense of satisfaction for what we had just accomplished. Our mission was to teach Unmukt a lesson and we had done just that. We had given him a taste and showed him that his actions had consequences. As we drove down the road, we laughed and reminisced about the events of the day. The drive home was filled with excitement and happiness as we shared our thoughts on what had just happened.. The thrill of the day was not lost on any of us and we all agreed that we would remember this day forever.

Sharp at 4PM on the day of the incident, I received a call from my father. To my surprise, he was already aware of the situation and was inquiring about the details. I was taken aback as I wasn't expecting that he would have found out about the incident so quickly. The call caught me off guard and I was unprepared for the conversation that was about to ensue. It was unexpected for my father to have knowledge of the situation and I was left wondering how he had come to know about it. Nevertheless, I tried to gather myself and explained to him the events that had taken place. I started to mumble, trying to explain the situation to him. I recounted the whole incident for him, recounting every detail I could remember. As I spoke, I could sense my dad's anger growing with each word. He listened intently, not interrupting me as I stumbled over my words. When I finally finished, he said that this was completely unacceptable." I could hear the frustration and anger in his voice, and I knew that he was going to do everything in his power to teach me a lesson and make things right for me.

Unmukt reported the whole incident to his school's principal. The principal called me and my parents to his school. The local SHO was also invited by the principal.

As I approached the door to the Principal's chamber, I noticed that my father was already seated inside along with the parents Unmukt. It was apparent that my father had come directly from his office to the school to attend this meeting. The atmosphere inside the room was tense, with everyone looking serious and concerned. I could tell that the meeting was going to be a crucial one and my heart started to race with anxiety. I took a deep breath and stepped inside, ready to face whatever was to come.

I was really nervous. I couldn't seem to shake the feeling of unease that had taken hold of me. My heart was racing, my palms were sweating, and my thoughts were scattered. I felt like I was about to step into the unknown and I was filled with uncertainty. The situation I was facing was unfamiliar to me and I was worried about what would happen next. My mind was filled with doubts and fears, and I felt like I was about to crumble under the pressure. I was trying my best to remain calm, but I was struggling to maintain my composure. I took a deep breath and reminded myself that I had faced challenges before and I had come out on top. I hoped that this time would be no different.

As soon as I entered the cabin, all eyes were on me. I could feel the anger and frustration radiating from the people seated there. The expressions on their faces were tense and irritated, and it was evident that they were not happy with me. The first words that came out of their mouths were scoldings and reprimands, and I knew I was in for a rough time. The atmosphere was thick with anger, and I could sense the tension in the air. I had never felt so embarrassed and ashamed in my entire life. The situation was completely out of my control, and I could only stand there and take the criticism.

My father had always been proud of me, and had high hopes for my future. He had envisioned me growing up to be a successful and responsible adult, contributing positively to society. However, when he found out about my involvement in negative activities, it shattered all his dreams and aspirations for me. I could see the disappointment and heartache in his eyes, and it was a gut-wrenching experience.Tears filled his eyes as he looked at me, and in that moment I realized that I had let him down. I had let down the person who had always believed in me, who had given me unconditional love and support. The thought of causing my father this kind of pain was unbearable.From that day forward, I made a firm commitment to myself that I would turn my life around and never get involved in negative activities again. I wanted to make amends for my past mistakes and prove to my father that I was capable of making the right choices. I wanted to show him that I was capable of becoming the person he had always envisioned me to be.It wasn't going to be easy, but I was determined to put in the effort and hard work necessary to make a positive change in my life. I wanted to show my father that I was grateful for all that he had done for me and that I was committed to making him proud

Later that day, as I was reflecting on my actions, I realized the mistake I had made by beating a guy. I was filled with regret and remorse for what I had done. As I was grappling with my feelings of guilt, my uncle and aunt surprised me by visiting me in the evening. They had heard about what had happened and wanted to come and talk to me about it. I was grateful for their support, but also worried about what they might say. I knew that I had let them down and I didn't know how to make things right. Nevertheless, I was grateful for their love and understanding, and I hoped that I could make amends for my actions.

VII

Piece: Impact of politics on your mental health

The mental health of individuals can be significantly impacted by workplace and classroom politics, which encompasses informal power struggles, rivalries, cliques, favoritism, and gossip.

One of the most pronounced effects of workplace and classroom politics is heightened stress levels. Constantly navigating social dynamics and trying to gain or maintain favor with those in power can be emotionally draining, leading to anxiety, irritability, and feelings of overwhelm. These effects can compound over time and severely impact mental health.

Moreover, workplace and classroom politics can result in feelings of isolation and exclusion for those who are not part of the dominant group, exacerbating existing mental health issues, such as loneliness and hopelessness.

Additionally, navigating power dynamics and cliques can make it difficult for individuals to concentrate on work or academic performance, leading to decreased motivation, productivity, and overall satisfaction with their work or school life.

Finally, workplace and classroom politics can create a toxic environment that can have a long-lasting impact on mental health. Gossip, rumors, and power struggles can foster a culture of mistrust and animosity, resulting in mental health problems like depression, anxiety, and post-traumatic stress disorder (PTSD).

In conclusion, addressing workplace and classroom politics is crucial to creating a healthy and positive work and academic environment. Employers and educators must provide support for individuals struggling with these dynamics

and promote a culture of respect and inclusion. By doing so, we can contribute to a healthier and happier environment for all

VIII

The Vande Bharat hero: Sudhanshu Mani (ex-GM/ICF Chennai)

Have you heard of Sudhanshu Mani, the IRSME officer from the 1979 batch, who led the team of engineers and officers that designed and created the Vande Bharat trainset? Despite being the driving force behind this revolutionary project, Sudhanshu Mani's name remains largely unknown to the public.

Sudhanshu Mani's remarkable career in the Indian Railways came to a close on 31st December 2018, after serving in various capacities, including his last posting as the GM/ICF Chennai. He took up the challenge of leading the team that developed the Vande Bharat Express, also known as Train 18, a high-speed trainset that would change the face of Indian railways forever.

Despite facing numerous challenges and hurdles, Sudhanshu Mani's team successfully delivered the first trainset in February 2019. However, the government and railway officials were not forthcoming in giving credit where it was due. Instead, Sudhanshu Mani and his team faced an inquiry by the Central Vigilance Commission (CVC) when the first train was trialed.

This lack of recognition continued when Sudhanshu Mani was not invited to the launch of the first train, despite being the mastermind behind the project. It was only after the new railway minister, Ashwini Vaishnav, dismissed the CVC inquiry that the team's efforts were finally acknowledged.

Sudhanshu Mani's story is a testament to the dedication and perseverance required to drive

change in any organization. His leadership and the hard work of his team have left a lasting legacy that has transformed the face of Indian railways. It is essential to recognize and celebrate the contributions of such remarkable individuals to inspire future generations of engineers and leaders.

Suggestion

For any improvements get in touch at **ayushranjan910@gmail.com**

9 798890 021113

Printed by Libri Plureos GmbH in Hamburg, Germany